An "I Am Reading Latin Stories" Book

Octavus Octopus

Octavus the Octopus

"I Am Reading Latin Stories" Series

Book Two

This is one of a series of Latin books developed for ages 5–8. Other books include

Ursus et Porcus: The Bear and the Pig **(Book One)**
Taurus Rex: King Bull **(Book Three)**
Rena Rhinoceros: Rena the Rhinoceros **(Book Four)**

Check www.bolchazy.com for more information.
Recordings of these books also will be on the website.

Why learn Latin?

A short answer is that Latin

- develops a person's English
- provides a solid foundation for the acquisition of other languages
- connects us with the cultures of 57 nations on 4 continents
- provides us with cultural roots and a sense of identity
- enhances our career choices

Latin vocabulary forms the basis of 60% of the words in the English language, and it also forms the roots of the Spanish, French, and Italian languages. The very act of learning Latin serves to increase the mind's analytic processes, and an exposure to the Roman world constitutes a journey back to the roots of our own Western heritage. It's never too early to start learning Latin.

An "I Am Reading Latin Stories" Book

Octavus Octopus

Octavus the Octopus

By Rose Williams

Illustrated By
James Hillyer Estes

Bolchazy-Carducci Publishers, Inc.
Mundelein, Illinois USA

General Editor: Marie Bolchazy
Latin Editor: John Traupman
Cover Design & Layout: Adam Phillip Velez
Illustrations: James Hillyer Estes

Octavus Octopus
Octavus the Octopus

Rose Williams

Bolchazy-Carducci Publishers, Inc.
1570 Baskin Road
Mundelein, Illinois 60060
www.bolchazy.com

Printed in the United States of America
2008
by United Graphics

978-0-86516-698-1

Library of Congress Cataloging-in-Publication Data
Williams, Rose, 1937-
   Octavus octopus = Octavus the octopus / by Rose Williams ; illustrations by James Hillyer Estes ; designed by Adam Phillip Velez.
      p. cm. -- (I am reading Latin stories series)
   ISBN 978-0-86516-698-1 (pbk. : alk. paper) 1. Latin language--Readers--Juvenile literature. [1. Latin language--Readers.] I. Estes, James Hillyer. II. Title.

PA2095.W56 2008
871'.01--dc22
                        2008024327

Octāvus Octopus in marī sub multā aquā habitat.

Octāvus Octopus in marī sub multā aquā cum mātre habitat.

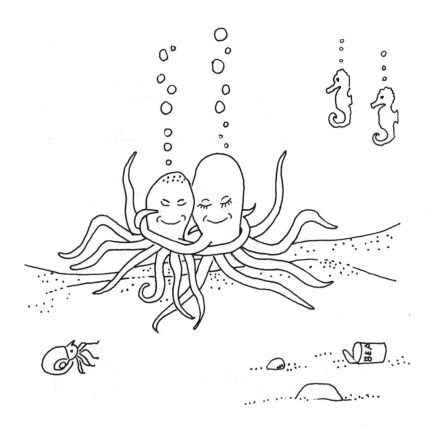

Octāvus mātrem amat. Māter Octāvum amat.

**Aquam frīgidulam Octāvus amat;
aquam frīgidam nōn amat.**

"Māter," Octāvus dīcit, "Pedēs meī frīgidī sunt. Soccōs dēsīderō."

"Tū pedēs nōn habēs. Tentācula habēs."

"Ita tentācula mea frīgida sunt. Soccōs dēsīderō."

"Octopī soccōs nōn habent."

"Sed sī octopī sunt frīgidī?"

"Octopī nōn sunt frīgidī in aquā."

"Sed sum octopus. Sum in aquā. Et sum frīgidus!" clāmat Octāvus.

"Nōlī clāmāre, cāre," dīcit Māter Octopus.
"Parō cēnam. Fortasse jējūnus es."

"Nōn sum jējūnus. Sum frīgidus," dīcit Octāvus.

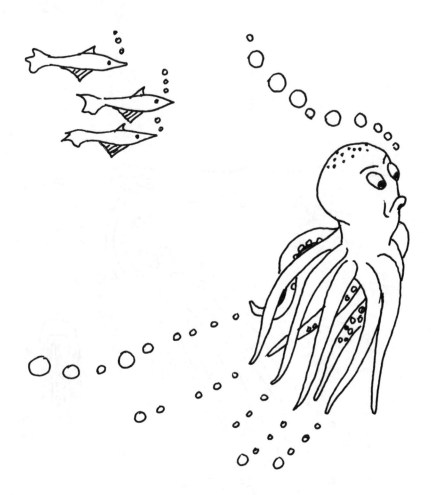

Octāvus in aquam vadōsam movet; sōlem per
aquam videt.

"Aqua vadōsa prope terram calida est," dīcit Octāvus. "Sōl est calidus."

Octāvus per aquam vadōsam celeriter movet.

Aqua Octāvum movet in terram.

"Ō," dīcit Octāvus. "Est calidum in terrā. Sōl terram calidam facit. Terram amō. "

Sōl est calidus, et terra est calida, sed sōl et
terra quoque sunt siccae.

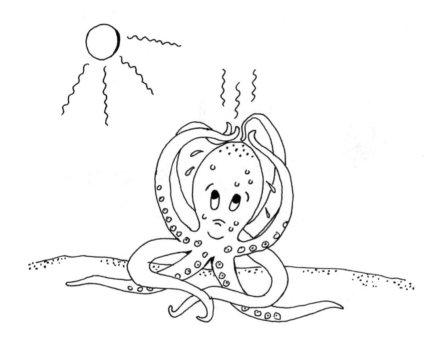

Octāvus nunc est siccus et īnfirmus.

Līberī in terrā lūdunt, et Octāvum in aquā pōnunt.

"Ō," clāmat Octāvus. "In aquā sum."

"Laetus sum. Aqua est domus mea. Frīgida aqua prō octopō est domus bona."

Dēsignā verbum corrēctum.

1. Octāvus Octopus _____ habitat.
   - a. in terrā
   - b. in casā
   - c. in marī

2. Octāvus amat _____.
   - a. mare
   - b. mātrem
   - c. cēnam

3. Octāvus est _____.
   - a. frīgidus
   - b. jējūnus
   - c. calidus

4. Mater dīcit, "Octopī nōn _____ habent.
   - a. pedēs
   - b. cēnam
   - c. aquam

5. Octāvus _____ dēsīderat.
   - a. soccōs
   - b. cenam
   - c. aquam

6. Octāvus _____ movet.
   - a. ad bonam cēnam
   - b. per multam terram
   - c. per aquam vadōsam

7. _____ sunt calidae et siccae.
   - a. Māter et Octāvus
   - b. Sōl et terra
   - c. Līberī et mare

8. In terrā Octāvus est _____.
   - a. laetus
   - b. jējūnus
   - c. īnfirmus

9. _____ Octāvum in aquā ponunt.
   - a. māter
   - b. līberī
   - c. sōl

Translation

Octavus Octopus lives in the sea under much water.

Octavus Octopus lives in the sea under much water with his mother.

Octavus loves his mother. His mother loves Octavus.

Octavus likes cool water; he does not like cold water.

"Mother," Octavus says, "my feet are cold. I want socks"

"You don't have feet. You have tentacles."

"So my tentacles are cold. I want socks."

"Octopi do not have socks."

"But if octopi are cold?"

"Octopi are not cold in the water."

"But I am an octopus. I am in the water. And I am cold!" shouts Octavus.

"Don't shout, dear," said Mother Octopus. "I am preparing dinner. Maybe you are hungry."

"I'm not hungry. I'm cold," Octavus says.

Octavus moves into shallow water; he sees the sun through the water.

"Shallow water near the earth is warm," says Octavus. "The sun is warm."

Octavus moves quickly through the shallow water.

The water moves Octavus onto land.

"O," says Octavus. "It is warm on land. The sun makes the land warm. I like the land."

The sun is warm, and the earth is warm, but sun and earth are also dry.

Now Octavus is dry and sick.

Children are playing on the land, and they put Octavus into the water.

"O," shouts Octavus. "I am in the water."

"I am happy. The water is my home. Cold water for an octopus is a good home."

Dēsignā verbum corrēctum answers.
(Choose the correct word)

1. C   2. B   3. A   4. A   5. A

6. C   7. B   8. C   9. B

Pronunciation Guide

Latin words generally have no silent letters. You can break the words up into pieces and pronounce them one piece at a time until you learn them. A slanting stroke follows the part of the word to be accented.

Here is a simple guide to how they sound. The long vowels are usually twice as long as the short; they sound like the vowels in these English words:

Long		**Short**	
ā as in father	Oc tā′ vus	a as the first sound in aha	a′ qua
ē as in they	dē sī′ de rō	e as in bet	sed
ī as in machine	ma′ rī	i as in bit	in
ō as in vote	nōn	o as in omit	oct′ o pus
ū as in rule	jē jū′ nus	u as in but	sum

Diphthong (two vowels pronounced very quickly together)
ae -ah- ē   (aisle)   sic′ cae

Consonants
Most are the same as English. Here are the notable exceptions.

c is always hard as in cake	ca′ li da
g is always hard as in get	frī′ gi dus
j is pronounced like *y*	jē jū′ nus
s is always hissed; never *z*	sic′ ca
v is pronounced *w*	Oct ā′ vus

23

Glossary

a′mō, a mā′re   to love, like   AMIABLE

a′qua, a′quae   *f.* water   AQUEDUCT

bo′nus, bo′na, bo′num   good   BON-BON

ca′li dus, ca′li da, ca′li dum   warm   CALORIE

cā′rus, cā′ra, cā′rum   dear   CHARITY

ce ler′i ter   swiftly

cē′na, cē′nae   *f.* dinner

clā′mō, clā′mā′re   to shout   EXCLAIM

cum   (*with abl.*) with

dē sī′de rō, dē sī′de rā re   to desire   DESIRE

dī′cō, dī′ce re   DICTATE

do′mus, do′mūs   *f.* home   DOMICILE

et   and

for tas′se   maybe

frī′gi dus, frī′gi da, frī′gi dum   cold   FRIGID

frī gi′du lus, frī gi′du la, frī gi′du lum   cool

ha′be ō, ha bē′re   to have   HABIT

ha′bi tō, ha bi tā′re   to live   HABITAT

in   (*with acc.*) into, onto (*with abl.*) in, on

īn fir′mus, īn fir′ma, īn fir′mum   sick   INFIRMARY

ita   so

jē jū′nus, jē jū′na, jē jū′num   hungry

lae′tus, lae′ta, lae′tum   happy

lī′be rī, lī ber ō′rum   children

lū′dō, lū′de re   to play

ma′re, ma′ris   *n.* sea   MARINE

mā′ter, mā′tris   *f.* mother   MATERNAL

me′us, me′a, me′um   my

mo′ve ō, movē′re   to move   MOVEMENT

mul′tus, mul′ta, mul′tum   much   MULTIPLY

nō′lo, nōl′le   to be unwilling, not want; **nō′lī** (with -re word)   don't

nōn   not

nunc   now

*oct′o pus, oct′o pī   *m.* octopus (Octopus is a Late Latin word derived from the Greek oktopous, meaning "eight feet." The earlier Latin word for this and some other sea creatures was polypus.)

pa′rō, pa rā′re   to prepare   PREPARE

pēs, pe′dis   *m.* foot   PEDAL

per   (*with acc.*) through

pō′nō, pō′ne re   to put

prō *(with abl.)* for
pro'pe *(with acc.)* near
quo'que too, also
sed but
sī if
sic'cus, sic'ca, sic'cum dry
***soc'cus, soc'cī** *f.* sock (Soccus is actually a very light slipper, similar to our slipper socks worn in the house.) SOCKS
sōl, sō'lis *m.* sun SOLAR
sub *(with abl.)* under
ten tā'cu lum, ten tā'cu lī *n.* tentacle
ter'ra, ter'rae *f.* land TERRAIN
tū you
va dō'sus, va dō'sa, va dō'sum shallow
vid'e ō, vid ē're to see VIDEO

Irregular verb **esse** "to be"

sum - I am	**sumus** - we are
es - you are	**estis** - you are
est - he, she, it, is	**sunt** - they are

Note About Latin Word Endings

In English the place of words in a thought or sentence is shown by order in which the words come. The subject and words that go with it usually come first, the verb comes second, and the direct object and words that go with it come last. In Latin the place of words in a thought or sentence is shown by how the words are spelled.

Look at the forms below:

Octāvus mātrem amat.   Octavus loves his mother.

Māter Octāvum amat.   His mother loves Octavus.

Nōlī clāmāre, cāre.   Don't shout, dear.

When someone masculine is addressed, the word for him ends in "**e.**"

The subject of a sentence may end in various letters, but the direct object ends in "**m,**" "**s,**" or "**a.**" A word following a little word called a preposition may end in "**ā,**" "**ō,**" "**ī**" or "**e**" if the preposition takes the ablative (abl.). A word following a preposition which takes the accusative (acc.) ends in "**m,**" "**s**" or "**a.**" You can see that the meaning of the preposition changes according to the accusative (acc.) word or the ablative (abl.) word which follows it.

Notice that the verb also changes. "**Clāmat**" means "he, she, or it shouts." "**Lūdunt**" means "they play." You do not say the word "he" or "they" since such words double the subject — Octavus (he) loves his mother.

Look carefully at the forms of "**sum,**" which means "I am." The other forms of **sum** will show you the endings for "you" as well as those for "he" and "they." However, the letter "**ō**" on the end of a verb means "I." The letter "**s**" on a verb means, "you." The word "**tū**" for the subject "you" is used for extra emphasis.

Adjectives (words which tell about the nouns) usually end in "**us**" or "**um**" if the word is marked *m* (masculine) in the glossary and with "**a,**" "**am**" or "**as**" if the word is marked *f* (feminine) in the glossary. Words marked *m* or *f* may occasionally end in "**em.**" If the word is marked *n* in the glossary, the adjectives end with "**um**" or "**a.**"

"I Am Reading Latin" Series

The four books in this series are for primary-age children: a rarity! Experts recommend that children start a foreign language as early as possible.

Features include carefully researched Latin, pronunciation guide, vocabulary with emphasis on derivatives, charming original artwork, special notes on the value of Latin, and an English translation. While children's books have been translated into Latin, it is rare to find any that are designed for students as young as four. Furthermore, the quality of the Latin would satisfy any classicist.

How Many Animals? Quot Animalia?
Marie Carducci Bolchazy
Mardah B.C. Weinfield, translator
Kristie Stock, illustrator
64 pp (2002) Paperback ISBN 978-0-86516-540-3

Children learn the Latin words and Roman numerals for numbers 1-12 and 100. They also learn the Latin words for a variety of animals, together with English derivatives.

What Will I Eat? Quid Edam?
Marie Carducci Bolchazy
Mardah B.C. Weinfield, translator
Michelle Fraczek, illustrator
64 pp (2002) Paperback ISBN 978-0-86516-542-7

Children learn the Latin works for their favorite foods: pizza, chicken fingers, hot dogs, and fish sticks. French fries and pancakes in a Latin beat!

Who Loves Me? Quis me amat?
Marie Carducci Bolchazy
Mardah B.C. Weinfield, translator
Michelle Fraczek, illustrator
64 pp (2003) Paperback ISBN 978-0-86516-541-0

Children learn the Latin words for family members: mother, father, sister, brother, grandfather, grandmother, uncle and aunt (father's brother and sister), uncle and aunt (mother's brother and sister), and cousins. The book begins with "Here is my picture," and the child gets to draw his image or affix a photo.

What Color Is It? Quo colore est?
Marie Carducci Bolchazy
Mardah B.C. Weinfield, translator
Michelle Fraczek, illustrator
64 pp (2003) Paperback ISBN 978-0-86516-539-7

Children learn the Latin words for a full range of colors: red, yellow, blue, pink, white, gray, black, purple, brown, dark green and light green. In the process of learning the color words, they also learn the Latin words for apple, flower, pet, food, bird, and canary. Finally they get to select their favorite color.

I am Reading Latin Series Audio CD
James W. Chochola
Audio CD (2004) CD 00002

Latin books for children ages 4-8 read in Classical Latin. This Spoken Word CD contains the complete readings of the Latin text from the I am Reading Latin series books. Including complete Latin and English translation text in liner notes.

www.BOLCHAZY.com

Living Latin

Green Eggs and Ham in Latin Virent Ova! Viret Perna!
Jennifer Morrish Tunberg and Terence O. Tunberg, translators
72 pp, original artwork of Dr. Suess, (2003)
Hardbound ISBN 978-0-86516-555-7

Dr. Seuss' perennial favorite, *Green Eggs and Ham* is here rendered in spirited Latin: in trochaic rhythm with rhyme in the last two syllables, a sprightly verse form that goes toe-to-toe with Seuss's whimsical drawings. Features include a rendition that echoes the lighthearted spirit of the original, the original artwork of Dr. Seuss, a Latin-to-English vocabulary and a note on "How to Read these Verses."

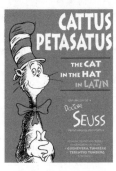

Cattus Petasatus, The Cat in the Hat in Latin
Jennifer Morrish Tunberg and Terence O. Tunberg, translators
80 pp, original artwork of Dr. Suess, (2000) Paperback
ISBN 978-0-86516-472-7
Hardbound ISBN 978-0-86516-471-0

One of the first books for countless children, this story of a free-spirited cat who, with his high jinks and mischievous friends (Things One and Two), turns the house upside-down for two bored children on a rainy day is retold in Latin in Cattus Petasatus. This edition features the original artwork of Dr. Seuss and a translation in rhyming verse that echoes the sound of the original *Cat in the Hat*. ECCE CATTUS! (For a teaching tip on using this book, to go to http://www.bolchazy.com/pdf/5564tip.pdf)

Quomodo Invidiosulus nomine GRINCHUS Christi natalem Abrogaverit, How the Grinch Stole Christmas in Latin
Jennifer Morrish Tunberg and Terence O. Tunberg, translators
64 pp, original artwork of Dr. Suess, (1998)
Paperback ISBN 978-0-86516-420-8
Hardbound ISBN 978-0-86516-419-2

The timeless tale of how the true spirit of Christmas captured the heart of the irascible Grinch is retold in Latin. This edition features the original artwork of Dr. Seuss and a translation that echoes the word play and rhythmic narrative of the world's best-selling children's author.

Bolchazy-Carducci Publishers, Inc.
www.bolchazy.com